Mollusks

Lichens

Sharks

Beetles

Diatoms

Geckos

Ants

Grasses

Humans

Squirrels

Crows

Dandelions

Coyotes

Earth, newly formed, 4.6 billion years ago.

UBIQUITOUS

Celebrating Nature's Survivors

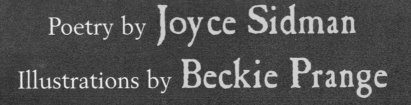

Poetry by **Joyce Sidman**

Illustrations by **Beckie Prange**

HOUGHTON MIFFLIN BOOKS FOR CHILDREN

Houghton Mifflin Harcourt

Boston New York

First Life
(a diamante)

Bacteria
ancient, tiny
teeming, mixing, melding
strands curled like ghostly hands
winking, waving, waking
first, miraculous
Life

BACTERIA

Kingdom Bacteria—3.8 billion years old
Average size of bacteria pictured: 0.2 microns (microscopic)

Nearly 4 billion years ago in the earth's oceans, life began in the form of bacteria—single-celled organisms able to eat and reproduce. These ancient bacteria arose from the mix of chemicals in the early earth's hot, acidic environment. As the earth cooled, bacteria gradually gained the ability to make oxygen. In a sense, we owe our entire modern world to bacteria, for without oxygen, higher life forms would not have been able to develop. There are more bacteria than any other living thing on earth. They are tiny (thousands could fit in this sentence's period) and they are everywhere: in soil, air, water, plants, even inside our bodies. Some cause disease, but most aid with important jobs such as digesting food or breaking down waste into chemicals that can be reused. In fact, without bacteria to help them rot, dead plants and animals would cover the world! Bacteria can multiply with astonishing speed (they can clone themselves every twenty minutes), enabling them to change— or mutate—quickly. Scientists must constantly develop new medicines to keep up with ever-changing strains of disease-causing bacteria.

The Mollusk That Made You

Shell of the sunrise,
sunrise shell,
yours is the pink lip
of a pearled world.

Who swirled your whorls and ridges?
Was it the shy gray wizard
shuttered inside you?
I hear he walks on one foot
and wears a magic mantle,
trailing stars.

O Shell,
if only I could shrink!
I'd climb your bristled back,
    slide down the spiral
        of your heart.
I'd knock on your tiny door
        and ask to meet
        the mollusk
        that made you.

MOLLUSKS

Phylum Mollusca, from the Latin *mollis,* or "soft"—500 million years old
Size of conch shell pictured: 9 inches (23 centimeters)

The thousands of shells found on earth—from snail to oyster—are actually the outer layer of small soft-bodied animals called mollusks. Mollusks have existed longer than almost any other animal group and are very diverse. In fact, more than 400 new species of mollusks are discovered each year! They arose when the earth was still mostly ocean, and thrived because their hard outer shell protects them from the various dangers of sea life: predators, injury, and extreme temperatures. Most mollusks hatch from eggs with tiny shells already covering them; as they grow, they add on to those shells at the outer lip. A layer of tissue called the mantle squeezes out the shell in liquid form, which quickly hardens into beautiful shining patterns (as in the conch shell, pictured). The empty shells we find are from mollusks that have died, sometimes eaten by specialized predators such as crabs or starfish.

The Lichen We
(after Siegfried Sassoon's "Man and Dog")

Who's this—alone with stone and sea?
It's just the lowly Lichen We:
the alga I, the fungus me;
together, blooming quietly.

What do we share—we two together?
A brave indifference to the weather.
A slow but steady growing pace.
Resemblance to both mud and lace.

As we are now, so we shall be
(if air is clear and water free):
the proud but lowly Lichen We,
cemented for eternity.

LICHENS

Kingdom Fungi— 400 million years old

Lichens pictured—in orange, black, white, green, and brown—are 7 times life size

Lichens are actually an ancient partnership between two groups of organisms, fungi and algae. In this very successful union, the fungus supplies a protective structure against the elements, while the alga produces food for the fungus (there are also fungi that pair with bacteria). Lichens are able to thrive in environments that neither organism could tolerate separately: severe climates like searing deserts or frigid Antarctica, or bare surfaces like stone or metal. They survive drought or extreme temperatures by "shutting down" until conditions are more favorable, and grow so slowly that some lichens are estimated to be thousands of years old. They are a main food source for animals living in northern climates where plants are scarce, and they also provide food and nesting material for many birds and insects. One thing lichens cannot tolerate is pollution; they decline in cities with poor air quality and forests affected by acid rain, and thus are an important indicator of environmental health.

SHARKS

Class Selachii—375 million years old
Size of Caribbean reef shark pictured: 5–9 feet (1.5–2.7 meters) long

Sharks patrolled the ocean hundreds of millions of years before the age of dinosaurs, and they have changed very little since then. Their long, torpedo-shaped bodies are superbly designed for underwater speed and agility; even their skin is made of tiny streamlined "teeth" that reduce turbulence and allow them to glide through the water, powered by the merest flick of their tails. Unlike the now extinct "armored fishes," which arose at about the same time but were weighed down by heavy bony plates, sharks are remarkably buoyant for their size because their skeletons are made of light, flexible cartilage. While some sharks eat only plankton, most are supreme fish-eating predators whose jaws bristle with several rows of teeth. In addition to having excellent sight, hearing, and smell, they can sense tiny vibrations in the water through their skin. Special sensors on their face can detect electrical impulses from the heartbeats of hidden fish! Although some species are in decline due to overfishing, sharks are amazingly disease-free even in waters filled with hazardous pollutants, and their immune systems are the object of much scientific study.

Protective coloring
Dark dappled back
smooth white
FinFinFinFinfin
Flick
Long Power-pumping bursts
Long lazy strokes

Scarab

Having
found me, you
are blessed. Born a grub,
cradled in rot, I am Sheath-wing,
beloved of ancients. You have never
seen armor like mine. As the sun-god
rolls his blazing disk overhead, so I roll my
perfect sphere of dung across the sands.
I lay new life in old: my young come forth
like jeweled warriors from muck.
From death, life; from ugliness, beauty.
This is the ancient lesson.
Learn it well. Blessed by
the gods are you who
hold me in your
hand.

larva
(growing)

larva
(full size)

pupa
(changing
into adult)

BEETLES

Order Coleoptera, "sheath-wing"
—265 million years old
Size of scarab beetles pictured: .8–4 inches
(20–100 millimeters)

larva
(an early stage)

Beetles owe their tremendous success largely to a single body part: their hardened forewings. In contrast to the flies from which they diverged millions of years ago, beetles' modified forewings act as armor, protecting their soft bodies and allowing them to live almost anywhere: in deserts, underground, even underwater. This modification led to an explosion of diversity into thousands of different species of beetles—many more than flies; in fact, more than any other animal group! Beetles pollinate flowering plants and are important scavengers, helping break down and remove rotting logs, dead animals, even dung. The scarab, or "dung beetle," was revered by ancient Egyptians, and its likeness made into jewelry and good-luck charms. This beetle, which rolls marble-size balls of dung to its nest, reminded them of their mighty sun-god, who rolled the sun across the sky each day. The scarab beetle lays its eggs inside the balls, which protect and feed the young as they transform into adults.

adult before
emerging

egg

pair with
dung ball

adult rolling
dung ball

Diatoms

Curl of sea-
        green wave
                alive
        with invisible jewels
                almost
                too beautiful
                        to eat:

in each
        crash, roar,
                millions
                        more.

DIATOMS

Class Bacillariophyceae—190 million years old
Size of diatoms pictured: 20 to 150 microns (microscopic)

Diatoms are singled-celled microscopic organisms that drift through the ocean by the billions, like tiny snowflakes. Hundreds of them fit on the head of a pin. They live in fresh water as well: lakes, streams, puddles—even Antarctic ice. Despite their small size, diatoms are beautifully made: each one is a transparent box of silica (a glassy substance) that protects the single plant cell inside. They have an astounding ability to reproduce, both by splitting in half and by releasing eggs. These abundant, sturdy organisms provide the single most important food source for marine life, from tiny microanimals to snails and fish. Even the blue whale (the largest animal in the world) depends on this tiny organism for survival; the blue whale's main source of food—tiny, shrimp-like krill—feed on diatoms. Some scientists say that through photosynthesis, diatoms—the "grass of the sea"—provide a third of the world's oxygen supply.

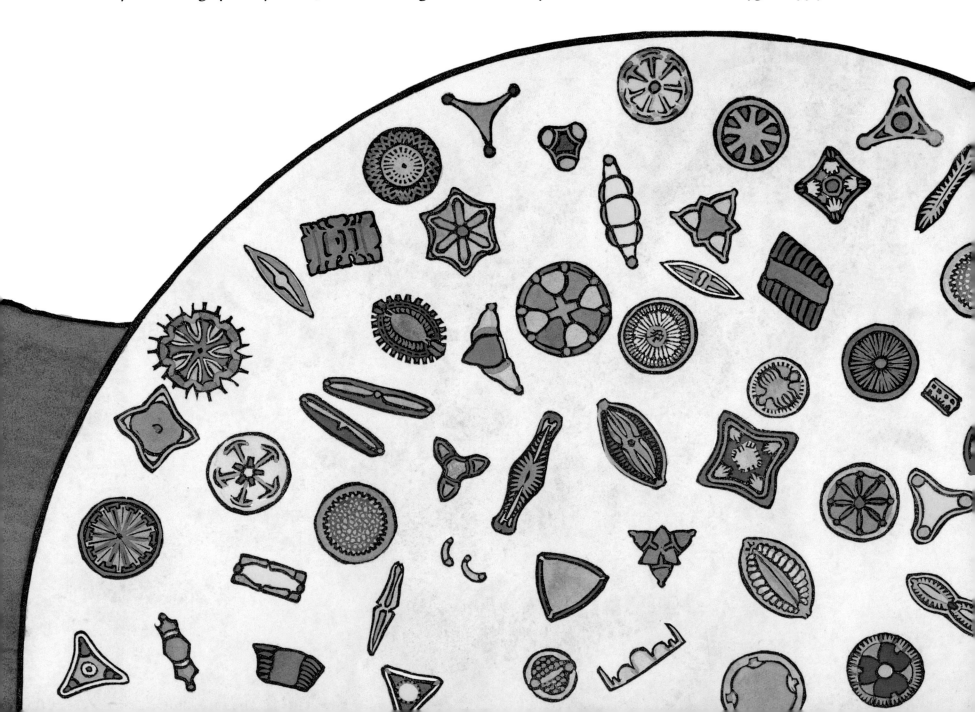

Gecko on the Wall

Her jaws dart out
      to crunch up flies.

Her tongue flicks up
      to wipe her eyes.

She climbs up walls
      with eerie cries.

Her tail comes off:
      a wriggling prize!

She sprints and leaps
      and slinks and spies . . .

Sigh.
Don't you wish you were a gecko?

GECKOS

Family Gekkonidae—160 million years old
Size of tokay gecko pictured: 8 inches
(20 centimeters) long

Small, nimble geckos are descendants of ancient lizards that existed on earth during the time of dinosaurs. They survived the mass reptile extinction 65 million years ago (the downfall of dinosaurs) and adapted to a changing environment by becoming mostly nocturnal—feeding on insects that are active at night. Geckos' sticky, hard-shelled eggs clung to floating mats of logs and were carried to distant islands, making them one of the most widespread of lizards. Many geckos live close to humans (even inside houses), feasting on the insects that pester people. Unlike other lizards, they "vocalize," chirping to each other to communicate in the dark. Geckos can literally break their tail in two to escape from predators. Since they have no eyelids, they use their tongues to clean their eyes. Scientists have recently discovered that geckos' toe pads, which enable them to climb walls and even ceilings, are actually made up of thousands of microscopic hairlike projections that cling to surfaces at a molecular level. Research is under way to develop a "super-Velcro" based on these remarkable toes.

The Ants

The ants, the ants
on tips of plants,
on sticks, on stones,
on ice cream cones;

beneath the ground
they ebb and flow,
precisely know
who's friend, who's foe.

They dig, they climb,
they drag, they haul
(they never seem
to play at all).

At obstacles
thrown in their path
they laugh! (Well, really,
ants don't laugh:

ANTS

Family Formicidae—140 million years old
Size of harvester ant pictured: .25–.5 inches (6–12 millimeters) long

Although beetles have a greater number of species than ants, ants win out in sheer volume: there are more ants than there are any other animal in the world. Some scientists estimate that the total weight of all ants on the planet equals the total weight of all humans! Ants live in every corner of the earth, from city blocks to desert wasteland, making their home in soil, rotting vegetation, and trees. Their hard exoskeleton and flexible three-part body allow them to slip through almost any small crack or opening. As earth's primary dirt movers and seed scatterers, they can carry loads up to fifty times their own weight. What makes ants the most successful insect in the world, however, is their highly

they just speed up
their antlike flow
and find a different
way to go.)

But when a gang
attacks their nest?
They beat their legs
against their chests,

they snap their
giant mandibles,
and drive them out
with great success.

And then, after
the fight has quit,
they go back home
to baby-sit.

*grasshopper
parts*

buckwheat seeds

pupae

wheat seeds

developed social system. Ant colonies can number into the billions, with each member serving the group cooperatively (and selflessly): building and repairing tunnels, scouting for food, caring for young, or battling invading predators (such as insect-eating mammals, beetles, or other ants). When faced with obstacles, ants find new pathways with amazing speed using a system of chemical markers. In fact, their methods of group problem-solving are so successful that large corporations study—and sometimes copy—their behavior.

Grass

I grow in places
others can't,

where wind is high
and water scant.

I drink the rain,
I eat the sun;

before the prairie winds
I run.

I seed, I sprout,
I grow, I creep,

and in the ice
and snow, I sleep.

On steppe or veld
or pampas dry,

beneath the grand,
enormous sky,

I make my humble,
bladed bed.

And where there's level ground,
I spread.

GRASSES

Family Poaceae—65 million years old
Size of grasses pictured: 20 inches–6 feet (50–200 centimeters) high

Grasses arose about the time of the extinction of dinosaurs, when the earth's climate began to cool and many tropical non-flowering plants died out. Helping to feed the growing numbers of mammals, grasses quickly diversified and spread. Grasses now cover almost one-third of the earth's land surface and feed much of the human world as well: wheat, maize, oats, barley, rice, and sugar cane are all grasses. Found on six continents, and comprising more than 10,000 species, grasses are the sturdiest of plants. Their thin, upright leaves protect them from overexposure to sun and wind. Their deep, spreading root system can survive conditions that destroy other plants—drought, fire, hoof traffic, flooding, and grazing. While specialized lawn grasses require extra watering and fertilizer, tough native grasses thrive anywhere there is a bit of soil and some sunshine.

maize　　*oats*　　*wheat*　　*rice*　　*barley*　　*sugarcane*

Tail Tale

OK,
your brains are
big while ours are
just the size of
walnuts which
we love to eat by
the way with teeth
that can chew through
any sort of bird feeder you
care to erect and believe me
we will find them no matter
where you put 'em being insatiably
curious and natural-born problem-
solvers just as we find the nuts we
cleverly hid last fall all over your
yard even though you let your dog
out at every opportunity
Sure dogs run fast but what
can they do in a tree
nothing
besides paw
the trunk and
stare at us hungrily
as we dash from limb
to limb sailing out over
the leaves with our para-
chute tails which by the
way also act as umbrella,
float, flag, rudder, and the
warmest, softest, coziest quilt
you could ever imagine oh yes
indeed your brains are bigger . . .
hmmm bigger brains versus tree-
top living with a free fur coat
and the ability to crack any
safe known to man now
really which would
you choose if you
actually had a
choice which
you don't?

SQUIRRELS

Family Sciuridae; from the Greek *skiouros*,
meaning "shade-tail"—36 million years old
Size of gray squirrel pictured: 16 inches (40 centimeters) long

One of the oldest groups of mammals, squirrels first evolved in North America and spread to other continents during periods of great continental shifts and climate change—when other, less successful mammals disappeared. One of the reasons squirrels thrived is that many of them adapted to life in the trees, where few predators could follow them. To this day, speed, climbing ability, and the world's most versatile tail enable them to evade midlevel predators such as coyotes or foxes. They are also omnivores, eating anything handy: seeds, nuts, fruits, insects, mushrooms, small mammals, and frogs. Most squirrels live very happily alongside humans, raiding food sources at will and gnawing with ease through wood, plastic, even metal. Squirrels survive cold northern winters by "scatter-hoarding": burying nuts and seeds, then digging them up later. Some of these nuts are forgotten and sprout into saplings—thus it is said that industrious squirrels plant more trees than humans do.

Crow

A single crow against the sky:
where do you wing your way, and why?

What message do you cry out shrill
to treetops cloaked in autumn's chill?

With coal black eyes and strutting feet,
what private councils will you greet?

What secret orders were you given?
What deeds to do? What plots to thicken?

What grand, colossal, crow-filled schemes
 take shape in your collective dreams?

CROWS

Genus *Corvus*—20 million years old
Size of American crow pictured: 17 inches (43 centimeters) long

Crows and their cousins (ravens and jays, for example) belong to the most intelligent family of birds, the corvids. Curious and adaptable, they have excellent memories and have been observed making tools, such as hooked twigs, to secure food—something only great apes and humans are otherwise known to do. Found throughout the world (except in South America and the Poles), crows have highly developed social systems and use interactive play to test physical and mental powers, strengthen relationships, and increase status. They play-chase with each other in flight, "pretend" fight, and even play tug-of-war with moss or sticks. They will often band together to attack or "mob" larger birds that prey on them. Multiple family units, or clans, often roost together at night in huge, cawing flocks that may reach a million individuals or more. Crows' omnivorous, scavenging diet and tendency to live in open farmland have made them close neighbors of humans since early history, and they are present in many mythologies. In recent years, they have thrived on increasing amounts of human garbage and roadkill, and have even been observed dropping large nuts at highway intersections so that passing cars will crack them open!

Fluff Head

Did you know
dandelions grow their hair
just as we do?
Each pale, silky thread
springs straight
from their head.

They were all blondes,
of course,
and each one
a star.

Now they can't
stand long
in a breeze
or their

f a i r y - h a i r

  f   l   e   s

DANDELIONS

Genus *Taraxacum* —5 million years old

Size of common dandelion pictured: 8 inches (20 centimeters) in diameter

A spectacularly successful flower throughout the cooler parts of the world, the dandelion was named for its jagged leaves, which resemble the teeth of a lion, or *dents de lion* in French. Unlike other wildflowers, which will grow only in certain environments, the dandelion thrives in any type of soil, wherever sun is available. First, it sinks a thick taproot into the earth, from which the plant can completely regrow even if snipped by a hungry rabbit or lawnmower. Then, once established, it spreads its hardy green leaves in a wide flat circle or "rosette," which crowds out other plants. Dandelions have an ingenious method of reproducing: each brilliant yellow bloom is made up of many small flowers, rich with pollen, which attract bees and other insects for pollination. After a few days, the flower head closes up and each individual flower develops into a seed with a feathery stalk. Then the flower head reopens as a distinctive white "fluff ball": a mass of seeds— each with its own tiny parachute—that fly off with the wind to populate yet another lawn.

Come with Us

Come, come with us!
Come into the woods at evening.
Come canter across the cornfields,
come slink in the dusk like smoke.

Come, come with us!
Come plunder the wind's riches.
Come drink in the hot odors,
come parry and mark and pounce.

Come, come with us!
Come kindle the blue twilight.
Come croon in the wild chorus,
come vanquish the tranquil night.

Coyotes

Canis latrans, "barking dog"
2.3 million years old
Size: 41–52 inches (104–132 centimeters) long

The coyote was originally a creature of the prairie but now thrives in virtually all of North America. It has spread far and fast partly because of the near extinction (by man) of its main predator, the wolf, but also because the coyote is extremely adaptable. To survive in different environments, the coyote can vary its breeding habits, diet, and social structure, as can many of its relatives in other parts of the world, such as jackals in Africa and dingoes in Asia. The coyote tracks small mammals with its excellent sense of smell, then uses speed and stamina to chase over long distances, striking when the quarry is exhausted. If food is scarce, members of a coyote pack will work together to outhunt competing predators such as foxes and bobcats, who hunt alone. Tolerant yet wary of human activity, the coyote has been known to eat garbage and even small pets in addition to its natural diet. As its haunting yips and howls become ever more commonplace in suburban settings, the coyote has become a controversial figure, viewed as both a threat to pets and livestock and a valuable predator of rodent pests.

Baby

Not small exactly,
       but soft, defenseless
Tremulous mouth
Clear, shining eyes

Grabs things and laughs!

Rises up on hind feet
but likes to be carried

If unsupervised,
climbs, builds, explores, creates, unravels
Leaves marvels
       and messes
              behind

Drawn to others of its kind
Loves fiercely
Plays elaborate games

Asks questions,
       questions,
              questions

and slowly learns
to answer them

HUMANS

Homo sapiens, or "wise human"—100,000 years old
Size of average adult: 5–6 feet (1.5–1.8 meters) high

Humans have been on earth only a tiny fraction of its history, but in this short time we have become one of the most dominant species of the planet. Our success probably has its origins in three characteristics: opposable thumbs (the ability to grasp and handle objects, a skill we share with other primates), an erect body that walks on two feet (leaving hands free for tool-making and carrying), and a large, complex brain (which developed language and problem-solving). While we are not as physically strong, adaptable, or prolific as some other organisms in this book, our large brains have enabled us to figure out ways of changing our environment—building shelters, planting crops, generating energy—so that we can survive in almost any part of the world. Complex language is perhaps our greatest achievement, enabling us to accumulate knowledge and develop art, culture, religion, science, and technology. We humans are also intensely social, creating highly structured groups that both cooperate and compete with one another. Our cooperative nature leads to acts of great kindness and compassion, while our competitiveness—combined with a tendency to crowd out other species—makes us one of the most destructive species on earth.

Earth today, home to more than 1.8 million known species.

Glossary

adaptability   The ability to change behavior according to one's surroundings.

algae   (Singular, *alga*.) A group of tiny plants having no true roots, stems, or leaves.

clone   To produce an identical organism from a single cell.

diamante   A seven-lined poem, shaped like a diamond, in which the word count is as follows: 1-2-3-5-3-2-1.

diverge   When two evolving populations of organisms begin to branch into two separate species.

diverse   Having a great number of different types (or species) of organisms.

domestication   The process of changing a wild animal, through breeding, to better suit life with humans (for instance, wild boar to domestic pig).

dung   Animal feces (poop), especially that of hoofed beasts like cattle.

evolution   The gradual development of living organisms from earlier forms during earth's history.

exoskeleton   The hard outer shell that supports and protects certain animals.

fungi   (Singular, *fungus*.) A group of organisms that feed on decaying matter by releasing chemicals.

immune system   A system in the body that protects it against disease or infection.

livestock   Farm animals such as cows, sheep, and pigs.

mantle   The layer of a mollusk's body that produces its shell.

mutate   To change suddenly and permanently, with the ability to pass on that change to further generations.

nocturnal   Active mainly at night.

omnivore   An animal that eats both plants and animals.

organism   A living being.

photosynthesis   The chemical process by which plants make food, which uses carbon dioxide and gives off oxygen.

phylum   A broad basic classification group of living things. Scientists divide all organisms into groups according to their characteristics and genetic makeup. The classification structure is as follows: kingdom, phylum, class, order, family, genus, species.

plankton   Microscopic plant and animal life found in the ocean.

pollination   The deposit of pollen grains on a flower, allowing the flower to be fertilized and develop into fruit.

primate   Any member of the biological order *Primates*, the group that contains apes, lemurs, monkeys, and humans.

prolific   Producing many young or offspring.

reproduction   The way an organism makes another one of itself.

social system   The system by which a group of organisms lives together and cooperates with one another.

species   The last and most specific classification of living organisms (see above, *phylum*). Members of a species look and act alike and can reproduce with one another.

ubiquitous   Something that is (or seems to be) everywhere at the same time.

For Carol, and the amazing, indomitable life force that she studies. —J.S.

Izaak Nosbisch, this one's for you. —B.P.

Acknowledgments

My primary, heartfelt thanks go to my sister, Dr. Carol von Dohlen, who was always taming birds or harboring reptiles as a kid and is now a biologist at Utah State University, which is no great surprise to anyone in the family. Her comments to me about beetles and their hardened forewings gave rise to the idea of this book. She has been unflagging in her enthusiasm, and has reviewed, discussed, and modified my work many times with her scientific eye. Thanks also to her colleagues in the biology department at Utah State, Mary Barkworth, James Pitts, and Kim Sullivan, who read and commented on several poems.

I wish to thank several other distinguished scientists who read drafts of specific poems and attempted to temper my poetic enthusiasm with scientific accuracy: Kellar Autumn at Lewis and Clark College; Andrew Ezell at Mississippi State University; Andrea Gargas at the University of Wisconsin; Allen Greer at the Australian Museum; Anne E. Martin of the Reef Quest Centre for Shark Research; Peter Raven at the Missouri Botanical Garden; Mike Sorenson at Boston University; Scott Steppan at Florida State University; Edward Theriot at the University of Texas at Austin; and Jonathan Way at Boston College. In the end, however, decisions on content were my own and I take full responsibility for any errors.

"Grass" first appeared in *Cricket* magazine, vol. 30, no. 11, July 2003.

The illustrations in this book are linocuts, hand-colored with watercolor.
The text of this book is set in Berling, Caslon Antique, and ITC Legacy Sans.

Library of Congress Cataloging-in-Publication Data is on file.
ISBN 978-0-618-71719-4

Printed in Singapore
TWP 10 9 8 7 6 5 4 3 2
4500223829

Author's Note

When you consider that 99 percent of all species that have ever existed are now extinct, you realize that the ones who made it—and are thriving—are indeed remarkable. This book is a sampling of such successes, arranged in the order of their appearance in evolutionary time. The first few poems are about large groups—mollusks, ants, grasses—that have diversified into thousands of different species because they developed ways of coping and thriving where other organisms failed. The later poems are about individual species—dandelions, coyotes, humans—that have been spectacularly successful for a variety of reasons.

To help shed light on the origin of these survivors, we have included a timeline. The question "When did a certain organism arise?" is not always an easy one to answer, however. All over the world, scientists called evolutionary biologists are attempting to date the evolution of certain organisms, and as they discover new clues, they must constantly revise their estimates. In fact, while this book was in production, the accepted date of ant evolution shifted from 100 to 140 million years ago. Therefore, any timeline—ours included—would need to be updated as new research appears. To track the latest findings on the study of living creatures, one wonderful resource is the Tree of Life Project (www.tolweb.org/tree/), a Web-based research tool created by collaborative biologists around the world and hosted by the University of Arizona. Another collaborative resource is the Encyclopedia of Life (www.eol.org), which was launched in 2007 and will attempt to create Internet pages for all 1.8 million species currently named and those just being discovered, including photographs, video, sound, location maps, and other multimedia information.

In addition to consulting individual biologists and studying scientific articles, I read many, many books to research this work. The most eye-opening were Bert Hölldobler and Edward O. Wilson's *The Ants* (Harvard University Press, 1990), Lynn Clark's edition of *Agnes Chase's First Book of Grasses* (Smithsonian Institute Press, 1996), and Candace Savage's *Bird Brains: The Intelligence of Crows, Ravens, Magpies, and Jays* (Sierra Club Books, 1995). I also relied heavily on Robert Snedden's *The Diversity of Life: From Single Cells to Multicellular Organisms* (Heineman Library, 2003) and many excellent DK Eyewitness Books, particularly *Life; Plant; Prehistoric Life;* and *Sharks.* Two other books I would recommend to anyone interested in evolutionary processes are *Life on Earth: The Story of Evolution* by Steve Jenkins (Houghton Mifflin, 2002) and *Our Family Tree: An Evolution Story* by Lisa Westberg Peters (Harcourt, 2003).

To find more survivor species, please visit my website at www.joycesidman.com.

Illustrator's Note

The timeline on the endpapers of this book arose from our desire to show, graphically, when various forms of life appeared on earth; my own ignorance of the vastness of geologic time and astonishment on doing the math; the relatively short time multicellular life has existed here; and the limited space I (and most other timeline makers) work within.

What you see is a string 46 meters long, with 1 centimeter equaling 1 million years, measured as accurately as I possibly could. (Cotton string is stretchy!) It is marked at changes in geologic period with a light spot in the line. Each timeline I have seen is a bit different in what it includes. This one represents the Archaean and Proterozoic eons and the Sturtian period, the Great Unconformity, and Vendian period of the Precambrian era in reds and oranges; the Cambrian, Ordovician, Silurian, Devonian, Carboniferous, and Permian periods of the Paleozoic era in yellows and greenish yellows; the Triassic, Jurassic, and Cretaceous periods of the Mesozoic era in greens; and the Tertiary and Quaternary periods of the Cenozoic era in blues. I hope it opens your eyes as it has opened mine.

Earth, newly formed, 4.6 billion years ago.

Bacteria

Scale: 1 centimeter equals 1 million years ⊢——⊣